I0765665

LOCAL BUSINESS TEXT MESSAGE MARKETING

25 THINGS YOU NEED TO KNOW

By: Jim Hayne

© 2019 Jim Hayne. ALL RIGHTS RESERVED. No part of this book may be reproduced or transmitted in any form whatsoever, electronic, or mechanical, including photocopying, recording, or by any informational storage or retrieval system without the expressed written, dated and signed permission from the author.

LIMITS OF LIABILITY / DISCLAIMER OF WARRANTY:

The author and publisher of this book have used their best efforts in preparing this material. The author and publisher make no representation or warranties with respect to the accuracy, applicability, fitness, or completeness of the contents of this program. They disclaim any warranties (expressed or implied), merchantability, or fitness for any particular purpose. The author and publisher shall in no event be held liable for any loss or other damages, including but not limited to special, incidental, consequential, or other damages. As always, the advice of a competent legal, tax, accounting or other professional should be sought.

TABLE OF CONTENTS

ABOUT THE AUTHOR

Jim Hayne is an American business marketing and sales specialist. He lives in La Verne, California which is 40 miles east of Los Angeles.

Jim Has had three main careers in his life. First, he had the opportunity to minister to young people as a youth minister for both Presbyterian and Baptist churches located mostly in Southern California. Jim did this for over eighteen before making a change to a new career in wealth management.

Working as a wealth manager, Jim helped both families and small business investors plan and invest toward their desired goals. After seventeen plus years helping individuals with their money, Jim has helped many companies as a sales and marketing specialist. Jim main focus is to move the needle in a positive direction for any person he works with.

While working in the wealth management arena, Jim was constantly approached by many so-called advertising specialist claiming they were the experts in delivering leads and he would have great success, if only he would invest in their system providing quality leads. One after another of these so called amazing lead systems failed miserably, and often delivered little or no results at all.

Realizing that success was really about getting new paying customers and clients through his door,   Jim began to grow his business by studying advertising and marketing and creating his own marketing of his design system. Systems work, but not all systems work for everybody in every location. To be successful, Jim learned that you have to keep an eye on any marketing process, to see if it has run its course, or needs a tune up.

One thing you learn as a youth minister is that you do not wait for the young people to show up at the church, but you must visit the places the youth are located and build relationships there. When Jim realized the solution to build his business was already answered in what he had been doing for almost two decades that put together a solution that worked.

Today, principals are the same, but methods may be a bit different due to technology. Regular mail and postcards through the post office has been substituted by email. Although mailings may have its usefulness because its stands out since so many do not use this method anymore. Personal phone calls have been replaced by text messages. Seminars have been replaced with webinars, and door knocking has been replaced with Facebook and other social media platforms. Asking for referrals from friends have even been supplanted by Google, Yelp and Facebook and other online platforms. Why the change? Simple, we can save time and get more feedback by looking at the reviews scores and even dig deeper and read the reviews themselves.

Technology has changed the way we interact with one another on a personal level and now has helped us with our shopping. Not all of the change is good, but most would agree it is the preferred method to interact with one another.

When we realize that currently Google is the number one source for research on just about anything, we know that Google is not going away anytime soon. Most Americans use Google to find suggestions and recommendations for the services and products they desire. Getting your business to be seen online is paramount to a successful business. It is no different then having a nice looking storefront for new customers to find you on a physical street, as it is to have that same customer locate you online. Having a quality website that is easy to find online is very important, just like having a business show in the Google 3 Pack would be in receiving new leads.

The quality of a businesses online presence can make or break financial success. Having a quality website that does more than hide in the vast information on the internet is paramount to success. Having a website that communicates effectively by first being seen, and second conveying your message in a way that makes your website stand above your competition should be a focus for all businesses. Having a quality website should never be taken lightly and sadly many small to mid sized business have never even created a website, much less upgraded from a slow and ineffectual site.

Most of what was shared above is about customers finding you on the internet, but what about the customers that have already found you, How can you reach out to your customers and retarget them to get them to visit you today! When you want to get a message quickly to your customers, you can send an email, but many of us have so many emails sent to us everyday, that we have become numb to an email chime. But one message most of us look at immediately is a text message.

When a business want to see fast traffic, they now will send out a text message or SMS to reach their past customers with a offer to help boost engagement.

This is why this book is written, to help share insight and knowledge with small to mid sized businesses on how and why SMS marketing should be utilized to help increase traffic from your past paying customers.

Jim has been called the Google Ratings Guy because of his knowledge and expertise in helping businesses repair their online reputation and teaching how to get quality reviews in order to if your business is not found with online searches. Having a quality website helps build your online presence and when created properly will deliver new leads through your business door. But once you have new paying customers, what are you doing to get them to make your service a habit in their life.

You can get a hold of Jim by calling him at Great Leads Local (909) 541-5987.

IS THERE A DIFFERENCE BETWEEN SMS MARKETING AND TEXT MESSAGE MARKETING?

Yes and No. Short message service (SMS) is text messaging done through mobile phones. Today, it is primarily done through smartphones. The terms 'SMS marketing' and 'text message marketing' can be used interchangeably. The main difference is how many texts you send at one time.

Another term, multimedia message service, or MMS, is another form of texting message marketing that many companies are using today. This services gives businesses the ability to send pictures and short videos to phones. Some text messaging marketing companies offer this capability, while others don't.

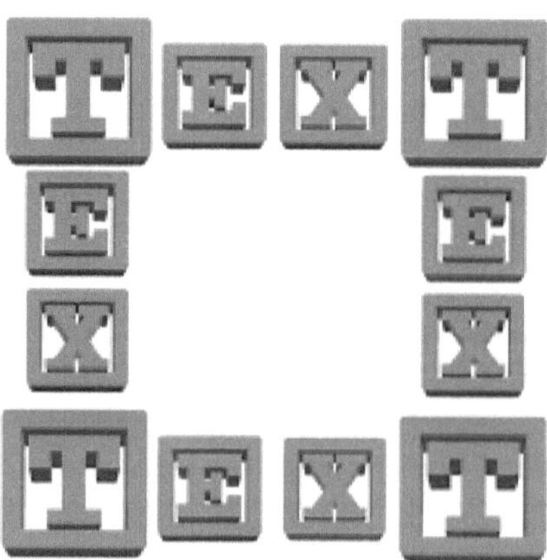

HOW SUCCESSFUL IS TEXT MESSAGE MARKETING?

In its early days, text message marketing was seen as possibly getting lost in the crowd in the world of digital marketing. Today, many companies use it as their main form of advertising, because it is more intricate than it seems, and has many benefits to both businesses, and customers.

The first is that over 5 billion people in the world have a cell phone. Many places that have poor communities with many without jobs, you will still find that most have a cell phone. That only leaves 2 billion people that don't have a cell phone. That's such a massive potential target audience for all businesses, no matter where they are in the world.

A text message sent by a business is much more likely to be opened than an email message sent from the same business. 89 percent of those texts sent are opened and read, which is much more than the 10 to 30 percent open rates of email marketing campaigns. When customers have opted-in to a text message campaign, they are ten times more likely to use an offer within that message than they are if they received the same offer through email.

The stats don't lie. Text message marketing is very successful, particularly when compared with other forms of tried and true marketing such as email marketing.

DO CUSTOMERS LIKE GETTING MARKETING TEXTS?

Another reason for text message marketing's success is that most customers love it! I would add the caveat that many people do not getting spam messages, but when a customer can opt into the marketing texts program, they do love getting savings and incentives sent to their phone.

According to a survey from GE Capital, 4 in 10 respondents said they'd shop at a retailer more if they delivered offers via text messaging. Customers are also twice as likely to take a survey by text, than they are by phone. In another study, 70 percent of consumers stated they wanted to be able to resolve issues without speaking to anyone.

It's clear that customers don't mind receiving text messages. When email marketing was first used, it wasn't long before spam became so bad that tight filters became the norm. While marketers and business owners are still fighting to get through spam filters, only a small percent of text messages are seen as spam.

IS TEXT MESSAGE MARKETING RIGHT FOR MY BUSINESS?

Text message marketing is right for most businesses. It's an affordable and effective tool that's become the norm for many businesses and customers.

Some businesses are hesitant to try it mainly because their target audience is not millennials. While millennials are the demographic that uses their phone the most, businesses that don't have millennials as their target audience can still find success with text message marketing.

85 percent of individuals over the age of 65 own a cell phone, says a study from Pew Research Center. And 46 percent of those are smartphones that certainly have texting capabilities. With stats like this, it's easy to see that anyone, in any demographic, can be marketed to through their cell phone.

Businesses unsure about the effectiveness of text message marketing for their business should ask customers if they'd be interested in it. Emails can be sent asking customers how they feel about receiving texts, or cashiers can even ask at a checkout.

WHAT KIND OF TEXT MESSAGES ARE BUSINESSES SENDING?

Maybe you already know what kind of text messages you want to send out. Maybe you want to start text message marketing, but aren't sure what you would send out. For any business owner about to start a campaign, there are many different ways this technology can be used.

It's a great time to invite customers to stop by during a big event. Restaurants can send customers texts about happy hour, a live band, or other special upcoming event. Let them know what the sale is, what the code is, and what dates the sale is on for. This is one of the most common ways text message campaigns are run.

Special offers, for specific customers only, can also be sent through texts. For example, a restaurant may send a 50 percent coupon to customers on their birthday. This can increase brand loyalty, while getting more customers through the door.

Flash deals are also very effective when sending texts to those in the area of the local business. For example, an hour before closing time, a restaurant may send a text stating that they have two sandwiches left and are offering them at 50 percent off to reduce waste. This creates a sense of urgency, which can be highly effective when used in text message marketing.

Sending surveys through text messages can also be very useful for a business. While many customers don't want to take these surveys over the phone, they are very likely to when it comes in the form of a text. Business owners can use these surveys once they're completed to make improvements according to customer's recommendations, and help make their business even better for customers.

Text messages that use behavioral triggers can also be very effective. Sending a message such as, "We miss you," along with a special offer can evoke emotion from the customer. This is what all good marketing should do, which is another reason text message marketing is so effective.

WHAT'S THE OPTIMUM TEXT MESSAGE FREQUENCY?

It can be tricky to get the right frequency of text messages down. You don't want to annoy customers of course, but you also don't want them to forget about you.

The general rule of thumb is that sending one text message a week is a nice balance. You can segment your customers so that only certain ones get certain texts, but ensure every customer is still only getting one text message a week.

The frequency texts are sent should also be tested and tracked. This will help you determine the right frequency for *your* audience.

WHAT TIME OF DAY IS BEST FOR SENDING TEXT MESSAGES?

There really is no one time of day that's right for every business to send a text. However, there is a general rule of thumb you can use in order to send the text during the right time of day. That is, generally, to only send them during regular business hours on regular business days.

This is particularly true for businesses that are using text messages to draw customers into their business. Still, only sending text messages during this time will also help with brand consistency throughout future campaigns.

HOW DO YOU BUILD A TEXT LIST?

Anyone that's run an email marketing campaign before knows how difficult it can be to build a subscriber list. This same problem can seem overwhelming when first starting out in text message marketing. Luckily, there are a number of easy ways to do it.

Using the reach you already have with email is a great way to start building an opt-in text message marketing list. Businesses acquire customer's email address in a number of different ways. Perhaps it's through a form on their website, while signing up for their app, or when the customer is in-store.

Emails can be sent to the subscribers on that list, telling customers about the new opt-in program, and telling them how they can take part. Of course, also tell them what benefits they will get from opting in.

Social media is one of the first places businesses turn to today when they want to promote anything. Doing the same with text message marketing campaigns can also be very effective. When telling followers about the text campaign, be sure to have consistent numbers and codes across all channels. Having different codes for different followers will only confuse your customers, and you when it's time to track the campaign's success. Also make sure you tell them the direct benefits they will get from a text message campaign that they're currently missing out on!

Contests and giveaways are great ways to build an opt-in list. People always want to get something for free and be a part of random draws. Promote a contest on your website, in-store, and on social media, but tell followers they have to opt-in to participate. A code can be given and once they text that code, they are entered into the contest. After the draw, you've gotten customers excited with one lucky winner. And, you have that number to use in future campaigns unless the receiver opts out.

HOW DO I KEEP OPT-INS FROM OPTING OUT?

Building an opt-in list is one of the most challenging parts of a text message marketing campaign. For the business owner that's worked so hard to get those numbers, even one opt-out can be discouraging. For this reason, it's important business owners know how to keep people from opting out, so they can continue to be part of future campaigns.

Business owners need to first keep in mind that customers like to know what to expect from the beginning. It can be annoying to opt into a campaign thinking one text message a month will be sent, only to later be bombarded with daily texts. When promoting your campaign, tell customers how many messages they can expect to receive. This will help retain subscribers because they are fully aware of what they had agreed to.

One of the ways you probably collected the numbers currently on your opt-in list was likely to offer customers a special incentive. This is not only beneficial when signing people up, but also throughout the life of your text message marketing campaigns.

People simply aren't going to stick around for something that doesn't benefit them. Offer an incentive, no matter how small, with every text message you send. At least once a month, offer a bigger discount, contest, or something else very exciting.

Also make sure that every text sent is short and simple. One reason customers love text message marketing so much is because it's incredibly quick. Keep the message short, telling them only the necessary information, and provide a link if they want more information. People will be more likely to stay on your list if you don't send customers blocks of text.

Using the right keywords can also keep more of your subscribers, because it actually makes it easier for them to use. Words such as "STOP" and "HELP" are included in most campaigns, as it allows the customer to make these commands automatically whenever they want. Customized codes though, such as "SAMMY", may be better at telling customers about a sandwich special and is easier to remember than a string of numbers. Customers like easy codes too, which will make them want stay on the list of a business that uses them.

IS TEXT MESSAGE MARKETING EXPENSIVE?

One of the biggest benefits of text message marketing is that it's one of the most affordable types of advertising. Bulks plans start anywhere between $0.01 and $0.05 per text sent. In some cases there may also be a monthly fee charged by text message marketing companies. These are typically $50 or less.

The question in regards to the cost of text message marketing isn't if a business can afford to do it. It's if they can afford not to.

One of the platforms that I like to use for local business does not charge per text sent, only a flat monthly fee of $99. I find many business owners like the knowledge of knowing how much their SMS Marketing Bill will be every single month during their contract period.

ARE THERE RULES ABOUT SENDING TEXT MESSAGES?

Yes! Privacy is a big issue today, particularly when information is being exchanged. For this reason, in 2012 the Federal Communications Commissions (FCC) declared text messages to be the same as an "automated call" regulated under the Telephone Consumer Protection Act.

Under the Act, businesses are required to receive express written consent prior to accepting text messages. This states that customers have to agree, sign up, or ask to be part of the campaign. In text message marketing, this known as an "opt-in."

WHAT TYPE OF INFORMATION WILL I HAVE ABOUT MY SUBSCRIBERS?

People have the strictest privacy standards today, particularly when they're giving out their email address or phone number. This can cause worry for business owners that have a responsibility to ensure that information remains confidential. The less information they have, the lesser of a responsibility they have.

The information a business owner will have after someone opts into a campaign will depend on how they opted in. Those that text a keyword to opt in will only be giving up their phone number to the business. Customers that have opted in through a form on a website or in their email may provide additional information such as their email address. This information can be helpful in future campaigns, but it is important the business treat any personal information they receive as highly confidential.

It seems that even the biggest of companies have fallen prey to the criminal minds that are able to hack into data frames. Many individual, maybe yourself included have had their credit card information stolen by no fault of their own, but because of a data breach incident. Because of these recent loss of personal information, it is important to do everything possible to protect the information, and never sell any information. This would be break customer loyalty and trust.

CAN TEXT MESSAGE MARKETING BE AUTOMATED?

Yes! Using text messaging software, the messages sent can be scheduled according to the days and times you want to send them. This makes it easier to coordinate with special events and promotions. Using this hands-off approach can save you time, and let you get back to running your business! Of course, these platforms do cost more money, but allowing you free to do what you do best, your business is worth it!

ARE THERE ANY SPECS, SUCH AS CHARACTER LIMITS, ON TEXT MESSAGES?

Anyone that's advertised on Twitter or Facebook knows there are often character limits placed on an ad. The same is true for text messaging, as well. A text can contain up to 918 characters. Remember, that is characters, not words. Any block of text longer than 160 characters will be broken down into blocks of 153 characters.

CAN TEXT MESSAGES BE CUSTOMIZED?

Sometimes business owners are concerned that their marketing material won't be personal enough, and seem form-like. Text messages though, can be customized a number of different ways to make them more personal. They can include the customer's name, or contain information such as order status, or a specific landing page on a website. Including this personalized information can help with the success of a text message marketing campaign.

CAN TEXT MESSAGE MARKETING BE INTEGRATED WITH OTHER FORMS OF MARKETING?

With so many different types of advertising today, it's never advisable to give up all forms of advertising in favor of another. The same is true with text message marketing. While these campaigns can be greatly successful, they should not completely replace other forms of marketing. Business owners can capitalize on their marketing efforts by using several different forms of advertising, and using each campaign to complement another.

For example, business owners could send a text directly to a customer, telling them to like the company's Facebook page to receive a discount.

CAN I INCLUDE LINKS IN MY TEXT MESSAGES?

These days, digital advertising is nothing if the customer isn't given a link to click so they can learn more. However, URL addresses often have lengthy characters and don't seem to naturally fit within a text. But it can be done. URL shorteners such as Bitly, Bli.ink, Polr, and TinyURL will shorten a URL, but still provide a clickable link to the content.

WHAT IS A SHORT CODE?

A short code is the code, or number, customers will text to opt into the program. Many platforms will use this type of opt in. This can be a string of numbers, or it can spell a word such as "BURGERS" for a restaurant offering lunch specials.

There are two ways a business owner can obtain a short code. They can purchase one exclusively from a text message marketing company, or they can share one with a number of other businesses using the same company. When short codes are being shared, the codes will be only slightly different to differentiate between the campaigns.

Some marketers argue against using shared short codes, as an exclusive code can be easier to manage and offer more security. That may be true for some businesses, but others may find the affordable cost of shared short codes to be the most worthwhile solution for them. Business owners will have to compare the pros and cons of each type of short code to determine what works best for them.

WHAT IS A KEYWORD IN A TEXT MESSAGE MARKETING CAMPAIGN?

When using keywords for many other online and digital campaigns, keywords play a vital role. They're one of the only ways to increase page ranking among the search engines, making sure customers see the content online. Keywords are important within text message marketing, as well, although they are used a little differently.

During a text message marketing campaign, a keyword may be the short code people text in order to opt into the program. Keywords can also be included within the text to create buzz, or link it with other marketing campaigns, such as an SEO-rich web page.

HOW CAN I ALLOW CUSTOMERS TO OPT OUT?

No one wants to think about, but under the law, customers need to be provided with a way to opt out of any campaign. Many companies use the code "STOP." A customer can text this at any time and they will be taken out of any future campaigns.

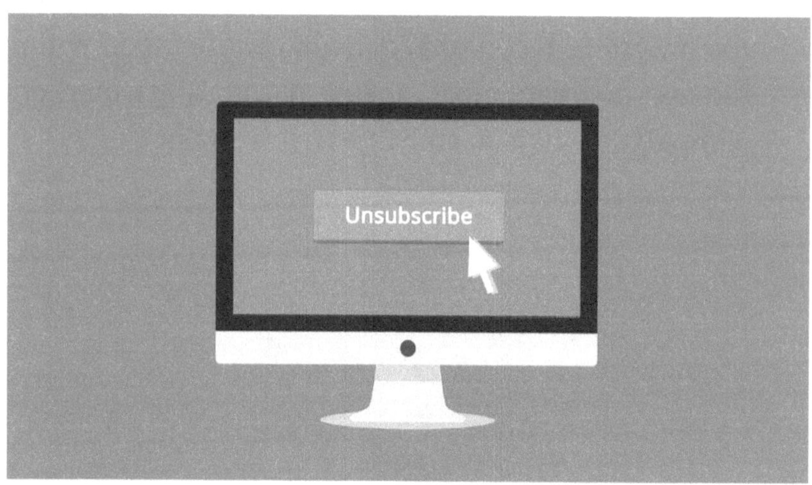

IF A CUSTOMER OPTS OUT OF TEXT MESSAGES, CAN THEY COME BACK AT A LATER DATE AND OPT BACK IN?

While watching the number of opt-outs climb during any campaign can be discouraging, business owners can have hope that they'll get those subscribers back again. Most text message marketing companies will offer a way for those who have opted out to opt back in.

CAN I SEND TEXT MESSAGES TO MY CUSTOMERS ON PRE-PAID CELL PHONE PLANS?

It's a little known fact in the text message marketing world that many pre-paid cell phone plans are not capable of accommodating text message marketing delivery for standard bulk short codes. Some companies today are getting around this problem by using technology that combines short and long code gateways.

Essentially, business owners that want their text messages to reach the largest audience possible should always check with several different providers first. Ask if they have the technology to deliver to pre-paid cell phones, and only use those that do.

CAN YOU TRACK A TEXT MESSAGE MARKETING CAMPAIGN?

Yes, and you should! You'll never know if a marketing campaign is working until you track different metrics of the campaign. There are a number of different ways to measure the ROI of a text message campaign.

Click-through rates are always a great metric to track, and they can be tracked in text messages, too. The click-through rate will measure the number of subscribers that clicked on a link contained in a text message. Analyzing this metric will provide direct insight into how many people are engaging with the content and interested in learning more about a brand or product. Google Analytics is a great tool for studying the click-through rate of any campaign.

The opt-out rate is also a good metric to study and unfortunately, no campaign is completely devoid of them. No matter how good a campaign or SMS software is, there will always be people opting out of it. While a certain number of opt-outs isn't concerning, a high opt-out rate is. It could indicate a number of problems including poor timing, not targeting the right audience, irrelevant message content, or too high a frequency of texts.

The conversion rate is the number of subscribers that take action in a campaign, divided by the total number of subscribers in a campaign. So if a campaign had 100 subscribers and 25 of them took action, the conversation rate would be 25 percent. This rate tells you how many customers took action after receiving your text. That action could be clicking on a link, replying to the text or a calling the company, or making a purchase are all desirable actions a customer could take.

The growth rate is another metric that can be tracked. It's also one that isn't often used with other forms of digital marketing. The growth rate indicates how much your subscriber list is growing. It's important that it is, because the more growth your subscriber list sees, the bigger your reach, the larger your audience, and the better able you are to position yourself better in the audience. To calculate this metric, subtract the number of previous subscribers from your current number of subscribers. Then divide that number by the number of previous subscribers. The resulting figure will tell you how fast your subscriber list is growing.

Perhaps one of the most practical ways to measure the success of a campaign is to calculate the cost per redeeming subscriber. After all, if the cost of a lead isn't profitable for a business, there may be things about the campaign that need to be changed. To determine the cost per redeeming subscriber, divide the cost of each text message by the conversion rate. If

the costs outweigh the profit the campaign brings in,
something about it needs to change.

WHAT ARE THE BIGGEST TEXT MESSAGE MARKETING MISTAKES COMPANIES MAKE?

While there's a lot that can go right in a text message marketing campaign, there's also a lot that can go wrong. Business owners can prevent this from happening though, by simply avoiding some of the most common mistakes made during these campaigns.

The first mistake to avoid seems obvious, but is one that too many business owners make. It's not telling subscribers who you are when you text them. When a text message is delivered, there's no way to display a logo or do any other real type of branding. Because of that, it's important every text message includes the name of the company. An easy way to do this is to set the Sender ID as your business name.

Another mistake commonly made is that business owners try to cram too much information into one text. It's true that you want to give your customer as much information as possible while you have their attention. However, long blocks of text are a turnoff for subscribers. They could opt out of the campaign because they don't want to read reams of text. The other disadvantage is that text over 160 characters will be split up into different texts, which will drive up the costs of the marketing campaign.

Failing to include a call to action is another big mistake made with text message marketing campaigns. Just like any other form of advertising, you never want to leave the customer or subscriber wondering what to do next. So tell them to click on the link for more details, call the business for more info, or to make a purchase while the sale is still on! Whatever the call of action is, it needs to be clear. If it's not, customers aren't going to go researching more on their own.

Lastly, the timing, or frequency, of sending texts can really trip some business owners up as well. Too many texts will irritate customers, so sending about one text a week is a good general guideline to follow. In addition to only sending texts during regular business hours on regular business days, think about what a customer may be doing at the time you want to send a text. Is your business open, but they may just be sitting down to dinner? Maybe wait an hour to avoid interrupting them. The chances are good that you know your target audience fairly well. You can use that when determining when to send texts.

SHOULD I TEST DIFFERENT ADS?

For every campaign that's run, there should be an A/B test. Without testing, there's no way to know whether or not a marketing campaign is working.

In order to complete an A/B test, two different ads are essentially created for the same goal. The ads will feature different messages, possibly be distributed at different times, and have other variations. It's important that the call of action remain the same. This way when metrics are being measured, you can make sure you're comparing the same information. For example, if one campaign asks subscribers to click on a link, it may have different results than one that asks subscribers to phone in because the goal is not the same.

Performing an A/B test doesn't mean that one campaign typically needs two different ads. It simply means that business owners should change their ad every now and again to determine what is working best.

For example, a women's clothing store may have different monthly sales. At the beginning of one month, a text message can be sent to customers telling them about the sale. Results can be measured at the end of the month to see if there has been an increase of customers during the campaign. The next month, the business can send the same monthly sale text message.

They can use different wording in the ad, send it at a different time, and compare the results in the same way they did the month before.

Each month for a few months, some elements of the ad can be changed. Over time, business owners will get a better idea of what's working within their ad, and what's not. Once they determine what's not working they can stop doing it and focus on the elements of the ad that are working.

NEXT STEPS

Thank you reading this book. We hope that you found it useful and that it has given you the information you need to help you better understand the importance of text message marketing and the strategies to employ.

We help many business both in getting new paying customers into their business, as well developing loyalty and teaching those customers how they can be the businesses best raving fans.

If you are reading this and are thinking, I can use help with this, no problem, we can help!

We would love to help you build a marketing plan that works at an affordable price. Simply reach out to Jim at (909) 541-5987 or go to greatleadslocal.com to get a time to chat with one of our marketing specialist.

www.ingramcontent.com/pod-product-compliance
Lightning Source LLC
Chambersburg PA
CBHW051128250726
48655CB00007B/2956